MW01265340

BREAN

BREANNA STEWART'S PATH TO BECOMING THE WNBA'S BEST PLAYER

By

JACKSON CARTER

Copyright © 2021

TABLE OF CONTENTS

LEGAL NOTES

WHO IS BREANNA STEWART?

Breanna Stewart is an American professional basketball player. She is currently on the Seattle Storm team and plays in the Women's National Basketball Association, the WNBA. She was the first pick in the 2016 WNBA Draft and is considered one of the best college players of all time.

Stewart has received plenty of awards and honors during her time as a basketball player. But how did she achieve these goals? Stewart had to put in a lot of time and hard work to achieve her dreams, starting back in her childhood.

This is everything you need to know about Breanna Stewart!

EARLY LIFE

Breanna Stewart was born on August 27th of 1994 in Syracuse, New York. She lived with her mother, Heather Baldwin. Her father was not an active part of her life, so her mother needed to work many jobs to support the two of them.

Her mom was her hero. Breanna saw all of the hard work she did while she was growing up and appreciated all that she did to raise her. Her mom would also support her on her journey into the professional world of basketball throughout her life.

While she was still very young, her mother started dating Brian Stewart. The two would get married later and Brian Stewart would adopt Breanna. She quickly started to see him as the father figure in her life. Her parents had a son, Stewart's younger half-brother, named Connor.

She was attracted to softball as her first school sport. She loved it as a kid but would soon gravitate toward basketball.

Breanna first became interested in basketball at a very young age. She loved playing the sport with other kids. Soon, it became something she was very passionate about.

BASKETBALL AT A YOUNG AGE

For most of her childhood, Breanna was playing basketball for fun. She wanted everyone who played with her to enjoy it as much as she did. At that time, Breanna did not know it would become such an important part of her life.

Basketball became a place for Breanna to learn and grow. As she fell in love with the sport, she realized that it was a great place to develop her personal skills. Along with the other kids, Breanna learned to work together as a team to accomplish their goals.

Participating in the sport also taught her discipline, commitment, and how to resolve conflicts. These skills would help her develop into the strong person that she is today and she would carry them with her as she continued to grow up.

When she reached 5th grade, Breanna realized that she wanted to improve her skills in the sport. It was at this point that she realized she would always love basketball, and it formed into a significant part of her life. Becoming a basketball player was starting to feel like a goal she would want to accomplish.

BUILDING HER SKILLS

Breanna was always tall for her age, eventually growing over six feet tall as an adult. This got the attention of coaches who wanted her to play on their teams. Most of the time, they saw her as a potential rebounder.

Still, Breanna first needed to build her skills in the sport. Her dad thought she would be able to succeed if she first improved her ball handling and dribbling skills. He suggested that she start a practice routine.

This routine consisted of Breanna dribbling around her block. She would usually wear headphones to make the time pass by faster, as she would usually travel the block enough times for it to be a full mile of dribbling.

Young Breanna would continue this pattern every single day during her childhood. Soon, she was able to handle the ball without much effort—her improvement was obvious. She could dribble the ball behind her back or pass it between her legs while she walked around the block.

This routine became a habit for Breanna. She would continue dribbling around the block every day throughout high school and even during her college years.

Now that she could handle the ball well, Breanna was again approached by coaches who wanted her to play on their teams. They could see that she had the potential to become a star player if she started in the game at a young age.

Breanna was picked to join her first basketball team at the age of 10. It was actually because her height stood out to the coach, although they would later see her potential and ability to practice and work hard to achieve her goals.

In 2017, Breanna Stewart would recount publicly the abuse she experienced between the ages of 9 and 11. It started to happen when she went to visit a relative. At the age of nine, Breanna did not understand what was happening to her. She was afraid and unsure of what to do.

However, when she reached 11, Breanna decided to take action and tell her parents what was happening. She gathered courage at 3 am one night and woke her family to let them know what was going on. They immediately contacted the police and the perpetrator confessed. The perpetrator later served prison time.

The events of that night would become hard for Breanna to recall. Still, she was very to have let her parents know. Later, as an adult in 2017, she displayed that same sense of courage in releasing an article on her experience.

Breanna Stewart felt that basketball was a fun escape for her—she loved playing at a young age. She was always practicing after school and throwing the ball around. Her parents enjoyed her enthusiasm for the sport and encouraged her to play when she moved on to high school.

The idea of playing in high school was very exciting to young Breanna. It seemed like the perfect place to make friends and grow with a team of other girls. She was sure that it was going to be an adventure for her.

However, it turned out to be so much more than that. Breanna was taking the first steps into building her basketball career, although she did not entirely realize that just yet. For now, it was a fun hobby for her to play with the other kids her age.

Stewart was going to move on to high school soon. Basketball had become her passion and she was sure she would be playing on the school's team. The sport became a space for her to grow and navigate the daily challenges that come with growing up.

She was ready and excited to play basketball with her peers. Her views on the sport, which she had during her early childhood, would follow her as she started a new chapter in her life.

STARTING HIGH SCHOOL SPORTS EARLY

Stewart attended the Cicero-North Syracuse High School. While there, she joined the basketball team under Coach Eric Smith. He was a good coach and would push Stewart to accomplish her goals. Smith also encouraged her to practice more, ensuring that she had the skills needed to play at her best.

Breanna Stewart would start playing on the high school team in the eighth grade instead of as a freshman like many other young players. The coaches saw that she had a lot of potentials and was way taller than all of the other girls. Because of this, they felt that she could start playing a little bit earlier.

The coach would have her as a starter for most of the games. In that first year alone, Stewart averaged nine points, about nine rebounds, and seven blocks per game.

Those records were quite impressive, proving her place on the team despite her age. Stewart felt accepted by the other students and was having a lot of fun while playing. Her team started calling her "Bean" because she was tall and skinny like a string bean and 6'10" due to her height and wingspan.

Breanna Stewart was having a lot of fun again. Still, this would be a place for her to grow and develop into a stronger player as well as a stronger person.

EARLY HIGH SCHOOL CAREER

During her freshman season, Breanna Stewart improved immensely due to her continuous practice and daily routine. Her scoring nearly doubled, with her scoring about 17 points per game. She helped her team greatly, making it to the final game.

For the most part, Stewart was here to have fun. It would not be until later that she realized she wanted to turn her passion for basketball into a full-time career. However, that does not mean she did not put her all into playing for her high school team.

Stewart was always practicing and playing whenever she could. Soon, this attitude for success would start to get her somewhere.

Breanna Stewart was working hard to get better at the game. She would soon be recognized for her hard work by her teammates and coach when she moved into the next year in her high school career.

Her sophomore year was intense as she continued to build her skills as a basketball player.

As a sophomore, Stewart was made the starter for each game. She would continue to improve, gaining more average points each game. That year, she recorded 22 points per game.

While she continued to play for Syracuse, Stewart noticed that basketball was becoming more and more natural for her. She started to feel like an unstoppable force on the court. Still, she stayed humble and realized that if she wanted to continue strong, she would need to keep working hard.

Stewart continued to work hard in academics too. She wanted to be sure that her parents would not change their minds about her playing Basketball due to her grades. Fortunately, they did not have any cause for concern, as she was bright and excelled at anything she set her mind to.

She would continue her daily routine of dribbling around the block. Many people who lived in the area recognized her, as they would see her bouncing a basketball outside every single day after school.

This routine continued to help her gain more control of the ball. Soon enough, she started to feel natural at that too. All of her skills were sharpening and she still had two more years in high school basketball to continue improving.

Stewart was excited for her junior year, which was approaching very quickly. She was sure that the next basketball season was going to be another adventure for her, and she was right!

Becoming A Dominant Player

During her junior year, Stewart continued to grow in stride. Her game had improved even further as she continued working hard. The more she practiced and played, the more she realized she had the talents needed to become a pro someday.

Not only were her skills improving, but Stewart was growing taller. She was a bit over six feet tall by this point, giving her an advantage when it came to shooting hoops.

In this season, she led her team to earn the state AA public title. The team won by 22 - 3. She would average 24 points and 15 rebounds that year too. Then, something unexpected happened—a college reached out to her.

The University of Connecticut, also known as UConn, noticed her skills as a basketball player. She was excited and responded to the school right away.

She would later announce to her high school that she was going to attend the University. Then, in a game the very next day, she scored her very first slam dunk. The crowd was in shock when it happened, then quickly went crazy. Everyone was cheering for her.

Then as a senior, she received official recognition for her accomplishments. Stewart was happy—she was doing what she loved and was improving every single day. The prospect of college excited her and led her to continue working hard.

Stewart was chosen to play on the 2012 McDonald's All-American team. The team consisted of the 24 best girl high school players. The selected players were then split into two groups that would compete in the All-American Game, which took place in Chicago that year.

Stewart would play on the 2012 Women's Basketball Coaches Association All-American, or the WBCA, team as well. The team consisted of the top 20 high school basketball players in the country. Since Stewart was chosen, she would get to play in the All-Star Game for this age group.

During the WBCA game, she would score a total of 10 points. Stewart was proving to everyone how dedicated of a player she was—it seemed as though basketball had changed from something she played with her friends for fun to something she was going to do professionally. However, to those closest to her, they knew this change did not happen overnight.

All of her friends and family knew just how passionate Stewart was about the sport. Now, she was receiving recognition and rewards for all her efforts.

Breanna Stewart would be named as the 2012 Naismith High School Girls' Player of the Year. This honor was awarded to her by the Atlanta Tipoff Club. Then, to top off the year, she was a part of a surprise presentation.

Tamika Catchings, a retired pro WNBA player, handed her the Gatorade National Girls Basketball Player of the Year Award. Stewart was one of the finalists to receive the honor.

This award had six girl finalists from various sports. Stewart was among them and was the only one who played basketball. She was chosen since she demonstrated plenty of athletic and academic achievements. Plus, she displayed a strong sense of character, making sports journalists take note of her presence in basketball.

Breanna Stewart was happy, excited, and proud of her accomplishments. Her family showed her the utmost support and was looking forward to what she was going to do next.

Outside of basketball, Stewart was also dedicated to her studies. She realized early on that school was important in developing and growing her future career.

She was an active member of her community, which also drew people to her. She would volunteer often for charity organizations. These groups included the Special Olympics, the Salvation Army, March of Dimes, the Ronald McDonald House, and many more. Additionally, she would spend time at the YMCA assisting coaches with the younger players and teams.

She would maintain good grades, on top of frequent basketball practices, as well as keeping up her daily dribbling routine. She even received the Cicero North's Outstanding Character Award around this time.

A NATIONAL TEAM LEGACY

Throughout her high school career, Breanna Stewart was also playing in the USA Basketball team. She joined the team at the age of 14.

U16

Stewart was the youngest member of the team when she first joined. Her parents had said "no" to the first invitation Stewart received since they were worried about her missing school, which could cause her grades to drop. However, Stewart was passionate about the sport and started to change their minds.

Mike Flynn, the director of another team, visited with her parents. When he explained that Breanna Stewart receiving the invitation was an honor, they gave in and allowed her to enter the team.

Despite being the youngest player, she was the tallest, standing six-feet tall. The team quickly accepted her and took her in. In this new environment, Stewart excelled. With her help, the team won a gold medal. Her parents quickly realized that they did not need to worry about her academics, as Stewart proved she was up to the task.

U17 and U19

Stewart would continue to play on the USA team. They would win all eight games and another gold medal in 2010. She had proven her worth and skill, landing a permanent position as the starter and leading scorer.

Stewart earned a variety of awards and honors during her time in high school, but soon, it was time to graduate and move on to the University of Connecticut. She was looking forward to further pursuing her passion and being able to continue playing basketball.

Freshman Year

Stewart continued to demonstrate great improvement right out of the gate. At the beginning of her college career, she scored at least 20 points in each of her first games. Her total amount of points came to 169, which is more than any other UConn freshman has scored in the past.

However, after her first 10 games, her average score started to slow down. Since she started averaging 20 points per game, Stewart decided she needed more training to succeed in the college sports environment.

This led to some self-doubt.

Doubts

During her freshman year when her average scoring dropped, Breanna Stewart started to doubt her skills for the very first time.

She knew that if she could not help her teammates win, she would not be able to help them with anything else. That mindset would stick with her for the rest of the time she played at UConn.

This was the first time her parents saw Stewart doubting herself. She seemed uncertain about everything, but her family was there to support and help her through this difficult time.

Stewart felt that nothing she did was working anymore. Then her father reminded her that she was there to have fun—basketball was her passion. Her parents called her frequently to check in on her and even got her an Xbox to encourage her to have fun again.

Her parents were constantly on standby. They were waiting for Stewart to ask them to and come get her. However, she never did. Breanna Stewart decided that she wanted to continue playing basketball with UConn.

Her confidence started to come back and she started putting in extra training time with her coach. Stewart's parents were proud of her choice to keep trying until it felt right. Soon, things would start to change in Stewart's favor once again.

But first, she had to put in the practice.

The Comeback

She started training very early in the morning with the associate head coach of the time, Chris Daily. He worked with her on shooting and taught her the skills needed to further improve her game.

That additional practice allowed her to return stronger than ever to the game. In the Big East Tournament, it was clear that she was putting in extra effort behind the scenes. She scored 51 points in the tournament. Most of those points were from the last five games, once again causing the professional basketball world to take notice of her.

Stewart was awarded the Most Outstanding Player of the Final Four; she was the first freshman to receive this honor since the year 1987. At this point, it was clear to everyone that Breanna Stewart was going to be the player to watch. Her coaches and teammates were sure that one day, Stewart was going to play in the WNBA.

During the first season, she quickly became dedicated to the team despite her busy lifestyle. She was untouchable on the court and it became a space for her to enjoy herself and get to know her teammates. They quickly became friends.

Stewart often thought about the role basketball played in her childhood. It was a way for her to learn conflict resolution, dedication, and working with others to accomplish goals, even as an adult. This made her realize that she still had plenty of growing and training to do within the sport.

Stewart was determined. She knew that with enough practice and commitment, she would be the one to bring UConn to the championships. However, she was also sure she could do much more than just that.

It did not take long for her to tell others in the basketball world about her plan.

Her Pledge
Breanna Stewart told the media that she planned to take UConn to four straight National Championships—the world was shocked. She had

mentioned it so casually, but something like this had never been done before.

However, now that she had said it, Stewart knew that she would need to keep her promise. That meant more training, practice, and playing as hard as she could during the season.

Her effort paid off once again. UConn made it to the National Championship.

End of Freshman Year
Looking back on her first season with UConn, Breanna Stewart would say that it changed her for the better. She felt that the struggles and challenges she faced helped her learn to be successful throughout the rest of her college career.

The losses she experienced that season are what continued to motivate her to this day. She does not want to ever feel like that again, so she plays her best at all times. This experience also gave her more confidence. Her team felt that she was more comfortable and self-assured on the court.

Still, Breanna Stewart was not done growing and improving herself. She wanted to continue to get better no matter how much work it took. Plus, she seemed like she was having fun again. Stewart threw herself back into the world of sport and loved it.

Stewart's sophomore year was quickly approaching. She was not done yet.

SOPHOMORE YEAR

Breanna Stewart had grown up a lot during her freshman year. She now understood what it was like to play on a college team and was familiar with what was expected of her. She started setting her own goals and knew that it would take a lot of effort to achieve them.

Stewart's hard work helped her to further improve her game. She was playing extremely well and her coaches took note. They felt that she was possessing the ball more often and seemed to be well in control of what was happening around her on the court. To Stewart, the entire experience felt natural.

Earning Awards and Titles

Her performance would earn her many more titles and honors. Stewart was chosen to be the American Athletic Conference Player of the Year twice. She would earn it this season as well as the next year.

Then she was chosen as the AP Player of the Year. Again, Stewart made history with this achievement. It was only the third time that a sophomore was selected to receive the award.

Breanna Stewart continued her training during the season, taking it as far as she could. She was willing to push herself to achieve her goals, and the results showed strongly. Stewart was chosen to start in all 40 games this season.

Stewart was setting records everywhere in the sport. All of her efforts was gaining her attention from the media, as well as the possibility of entering the WNBA. Stewart was excited that her hard work was paying off. However, she knew she could not stop here. Stewart was determined to continue to improve her skills and become the best woman player.

Stewart had left all of her self-doubts behind as her junior year approached. She now knew that she had what it took to succeed in a pro basketball career.

Breanna Stewart was confident now, something that her teammates noticed right away. They appreciated the steady change and growth she was showing and always did their best to help her along when she needed it.

Now, the next season for UConn was about to start. Breanna Stewart was ready and excited to begin. She knew that this was going to be another great year for her and her team.

JUNIOR YEAR

Stewart was feeling extremely ready and prepared for this season. As a result, she pushed herself even further, gaining plenty of experience and training in the sport. Her teammates loved her and started referring to her as "Stewie".

Her coaches felt as though she was still a kid having fun, despite demonstrating how talented and hardworking she was in the sport. Her father told her it was alright to celebrate her victories, although Stewart tended to do this her own way. Most of the time, her actions came across as being very casual, although they were actually very impressive feats she was accomplishing.

She would go into her senior year in 11th place on the UConn all-time scoring list. Stewart had achieved 1,960 points. She was also in fifth place on UConn's blocked shots list, with 288 blocked shots. Finally, she also accumulated 856 career rebounds, earning herself the 10th place with rebounds in UConn history.

Rio Olympics

In 2016, USA Basketball chose Breanna Stewart to represent the country at the Summer Olympics in Rio.

She would go on to say that it was one of the most monumental moments in her career. When her team won the gold medal and it was placed around her neck, the feeling was indescribable. She had represented the States at the highest possible level and won.

Stewart was a natural winner, but she never lost her head. She was always playing for fun and to better herself. This mindset continued to prove useful as she became better and better at the sport.

Me Too Story

The story she published on her abuse experience as a child captivated many people. She had shared a deep and personal story about herself. Stewart was inspired by the *Me Too* movement and McKayla Maroney to share her own experiences.

It was hard for her to share but Stewart was glad she did. Every time she told the story, she said she felt a little better about what had happened in her past.

After sharing the story, Stewart felt her life improve. The heavy weight she had been carrying on her shoulders for years was finally starting to disappear. Plus, she felt stronger after sharing her story. Her fans were able to see her most authentic self, and Breanna Stewart was proud.

She knew that her story had touched many women in a positive way. It helped and impacted so many people since they felt less alone after reading about her experiences as a child.

SENIOR YEAR

This would be Breanna Stewart's final season at UConn. She was excited to see where all of her hard work was going to take her. There were rumors going around that the WNBA was heavily considering her for their upcoming draft. However, Stewart did not let the idea get into her head.

More Successes

Instead, she continued putting out amazing results. She scored another career-high that season with about 9 rebounds, 4 assists, and 126 blocks per game. She also shot 57.9% from the floor. Stewart once again displayed amazing improvements on the court. The star's hard effort would win her another College Player of the Year award. Plus, the Wade Trophy and the Associated Press Women's College Basketball Player of the Year awards were also presented to her.

But Stewart did not stop there. She continued winning and would receive the American Athletic Player of the Year honor for the third time. She would be the first women player to be chosen unanimously for the AP Player of the Year as well.

National Championship

Breanna Stewart once again took UConn to the National Championship. This would be the fourth straight championship she went to. The pro world of basketball was impressed; Stewart had done exactly what she said she was going to do as a freshman.

Stewart had gone to four straight championships.

This made her a part of the first four-time championship class in NCAA history. As a result, she became the first basketball player to be named the Final Four Most Outstanding Player four times. During her college career with UConn, she had won 151 games, losing only five.

More Career Highs

Stewart was having a lot of fun too. Her coaches would fondly talk about how she always reminded them of a kid playing the sport; she would clap and beam whenever she did something good on the court. Her attitude helped her teammates enjoy the sport as much as she did.

And her work paid off too. By the end of her college career, she had at least 1,000 points and 1,000 rebounds to her name. This enabled her to finish her time at UConn as their second-highest scoring player of all time.

Breanna Stewart had gathered 2,676 career points, 414 blocks, and 1,179 career rebounds. She took the top spot at UConn for blocks too.

Something interesting happened during the championships as well; Stewart learned that she would be playing against the Orange team from Syracuse. That was the team from her hometown, one that she had heavily considered joining in the past.

When UConn won against the Orange, everything felt complete to Stewart. She had wrapped up her college career exactly as she wanted. She fulfilled her promise to bring the team to four consecutive championships. Plus, she got to face her hometown team in the finals.

For Stewart, this was the perfect college career. Not much could have gone better for her.

A Perfect College Career

Breanna Stewart had a near-perfect college career with the UConn team. No doubt that it was due to her hard work and natural talent, but it still was a unique and successful experience.

Stewart has become the greatest player in Huskies' history. Plus, the career that she completed while working with them would be just about impossible for anyone to recreate.

Then, during the final game of the season, she got to face her hometown team. Stewart was excited. How many people get to have such an amazing career ending by playing against the team from the town they grew up in?

UConn won; they scored 82 points compared to the Orange's 51. Stewart would score 24 points during that game, as well as 10 rebounds, six assists, and two blocks. It was clear that she did not hold back just because she was playing against her hometown team.

Still, she was surprised they were her opponents for the evening, but that did not stop her from playing very well.

After that final game, Stewart became the only woman basketball player to have at least 400 blocks and 400 assists during her college career. She is the only person to have reached 300 in both aspects, making it quite clear how talented and skillful she is.

By the end of her final season at UConn, Breanna Stewart was second on UConn's score list. The only person above her was Maya Moore. However, Stewart had accomplished a lot during her time at the college. Her career would be an impossible act for any other player to follow.

Her Advice

Breanna Stewart is a strong and powerful player. She reached that height by practicing daily and not letting anything or anyone else get in the way of her goals. Stewart would tell those looking up to her to never stop trying to achieve their dreams.

Because she was able to stick to her goals, Breanna Stewart had transformed into the greatest college basketball player. But what was she going to do next? The world was watching her with great anticipation as the women's Draft started to approach. Would Stewart be joining the ranks of the WNBA?

The Senior Ceremony

As per UConn tradition, at the final game, they have a night dedicated to the seniors. Breanna Stewart's family was extremely proud of her. Her mother and father were ready to walk with her across the court at the Gampel Pavilion. The three would hold hands and walk as the crowd cheered.

It was a major moment in Stewart's life. It was a celebration of the amazing career she had at UConn. Her parents were excited, happy, and emotional throughout the ceremony.

They remembered a time when Stewart was uncertain of her basketball skills—when she was a young kid. But she had practiced and worked hard to train her talents. The confidence had come with that practice as well.

Now, she was about to graduate. It was a very important moment for her. Stewart had accomplished earning a Bachelor's degree in Sport in Society studies.

During the ceremony, she took the microphone without hesitation and told the crowd at the pavilion that she was very grateful for all their support. She told them that she was not done yet, leaving everyone excited and wondering what she would do next in her basketball journey.

THE DRAFT

Breanna Stewart was now well known in the WNBA. She had led UConn to great successes and she had found out that she was going to be in the 2016 Draft. Everything she had been working for in her college and even high school careers had led up to this moment.

On the night of the Draft, Breanna Stewart was filmed and photographed by the media. She wore a red jumpsuit that gave her confidence as she sat with her parents. The outfit was a last-minute choice, but she loved it.

The outfit was custom-made just for her by the designer, Roland Mouret, who was introduced to Stewart through her agent. The interaction made her even more excited for the Draft night.

As Stewart waited with her parents for the WNBA president, Lisa Borders, to call her name, the media continued to give her attention. Everyone wanted pictures of Breanna Stewart!

Being Chosen

It did not take long for Breanna Stewart's name to be called. She actually knew which team was going to pick her. When the Draft lottery was conducted, Seattle won the first pick. They immediately said they were going to choose Stewart.

The team leaders were excited and relieved when they won the lottery. It was basically a ticket to obtain the best player in women's college basketball. If they had not gotten the first pick, it was unlikely that Seattle would have secured Stewart for themselves.

Seattle was going to be a long way from her home in Syracuse, but Stewart was excited. She knew the new experiences would be good for her and she mentioned that she was looking forward to a change in scenery.

Breanna Stewart was now the number one WNBA 2016 Draft pick. She would be joining the Storm, which is the basketball team based in Seattle. Being the first one drafted, she realized she was going to have a lot of expectations to live up to.

Luckily, she knew she would be able to handle them.

INTO THE BIG TIME

Breanna Stewart was the top pick in the WNBA, which is no small feat. She was going to be a huge asset to the Storm, if her performance during her college career was any indication of the type of player she was.

By this point, Stewart had finished growing. She had reached over six-feet tall. Plus, she had an outstanding seven-foot-one wingspan. This is incredible, as LeBron James does not even have that reach; his wingspan is seven feet.

This would give her quite the advantage over many of the other players. Her jump shot was powerful and on release, she could reach over nine feet. At that height, it was extremely difficult (if not completely impossible) for defenders to stop the ball.

Now, Stewart was going to take her skills into the WNBA.

After the draft, Stewart spent a lot of time doing photoshoots, with her parents patiently waiting for her to be finished. All eyes were on her in the sports world. While she experienced receiving attention in high school and college, this was much more.

People were treating her like a star.

The impact of this event made Breanna Stewart realize just what she was in for. Expectations for her performances in the WNBA were high—now she realized just how high they were.

She was going to become the face of the league, even if she currently had no idea what was about to happen to her. Still, some people had their doubts about Breanna Stewart and she knew that she was going to have to put in a lot of effort to prove them wrong.

Everyone wanted her to be the one that boosted the WNBA's TV ratings, which was a lot of expectations for a rookie to live up to at the time. Not many people were giving the WNBA the attention it deserved, and leaders were expecting her to change the situation.

She was a quiet but confident rookie with an amazing record in college basketball. Plus, it seemed like everything was going to keep getting better and better for her from here on. Stewart realized that being in the league was going to take a lot of effort, dedication, and hard work on her part.

Stewart later mentioned that she felt as though the draft signaled hope for the franchise. It was about what players were going to make the year and upcoming seasons better.

Luckily for the Storm, Stewart was going to prove that she is a very valuable player to have on a team

Rookie Year 2016

Breanna Stewart would be playing alongside the star point guard, Sue Bird. Stewart was excited to meet her and even more excited to be on the veteran's team.

Stewart would make a huge impact right away during her rookie season. In her debut game against the Los Angeles Sparks, Stewart scored 23 points. The season continued much the same way, with Stewart gaining more and more offensive traction as time went on.

Stewart would go on to score a career-high of 38 points against the Atlanta Dream, leading her team to a victory. To Stewart, it seemed like she fit right in with the other women players. They all worked together to achieve their goals. She was deeply looking forward to where her career would take her next.

During her rookie season, Stewart would average 18.3 points, 1.8 blocks, and 9.3 rebounds a game. Because of her amazing display of talent, she took home many Rookie of the Month Awards.

In fact, she would win them practically every month. The leaders at the WNBA were greatly impressed by her talents as well as her ability to work hard to accomplish anything she set her mind to.

Her performance during this season would lead the Storm into the playoffs; the team was very happy that they had Stewart on their side. It would be the Storm's first time making it to the playoffs in three years, so they knew they would have to play at their best.

Sadly, the team lost in the first round to the Atlanta Dream. The loss disappointed Stewart but it gave her even more motivation to continue with her training.

By the end of her rookie season, Stewart won the 2016 ESPY Award for the Best Woman Athlete.

Rookie of the Year

This was another title that she would add to her long list of awards. As part of the honor of winning the award, which was to be presented by Samsung, Stewart would receive $5,000. The trophy given to her was designed by Tiffany & Co. as well.

Stewart was thrilled. This was a significant achievement for her personal career.

Now, everyone in the WNBA was aware of what this amazing player could accomplish. Her rookie season was one of the best ever recorded in the history of the WNBA. Once again, she was displaying her natural skills, but also those she developed through years of hard work and practice.

She quickly formed a duo on the court with Jewell Loyd, who happened to be the number one pick in the previous year's Draft and the last Rookie of the Year. The two worked extremely well together, each pushing the other to succeed. They would become a mini team within the Storm.

Ending Her Rookie Season

All eyes were on Breanna Stewart. She displayed a lot of confidence and was winning awards and honors left and right. The WNBA was again impressed with her talent and skill. As she trained for the next season, everyone was looking forward to seeing how she would perform.

Stewart knew that she would need to push herself if she wanted to truly flourish in the WNBA. She trained as hard as she could, looking for ways to further her successes as a basketball player.

Breanna Stewart would not rest; she wanted to continue playing while she waited for the next season to start. She would accept an offer from Shanghai Baoshan Dahua to play in the WCBA for the 2016 to 2017 season in China.

She would return to play with the team again in 2017 for the following season. Then during each season break, she would play overseas. However, in June 2018, she signed with the Dynamo Kursk of the Russian Premier League instead.

Becoming An All Star

In 2017, Stewart demonstrated impressive growth after an amazing rookie season. Because of all her efforts, she was chosen to play in the 2017 WNBA All-Star Game. This would be her first WNBA career appearance as an All-Star player.

Again, she led the team to the playoffs. But like the season before, they were stopped in the first round of eliminations. This time, the Storm was knocked out of the competition by the Phoenix Mercury. They finished as the number eight seed in the league.

Although she was disappointed again, Stewart now had to focus on the All-Star Game.

All-Star 2017 Game
Breanna Stewart was going to be a reserve player for the Western Conference. The game was to take place in Seattle and was going to be on TV. Stewart was a bit nervous, but that was quickly replaced by excitement.

She felt that it was a real honor to be chosen as an All-Star player. That also meant that she was going to represent her team well. Going to an All-Star game was one of the highest goals of professional players, so Stewart wanted to make the experience count.

The contest would end with the Western Conference beating the Eastern Conference. The win was somewhat close at 130 to 121. Maya Moore was named the MVP and the competition ended. Stewart was extremely grateful for the experience she gained during this time.

She knew she would need it as she furthered her career in the WNBA.

An MVP and a Championship

Breanna Stewart still continued to improve. She was selected for another All-Star Game, where she would make her second straight appearance. By the time the season ended, Stewart would be second in the league for points scored. Plus, she continued hitting career-highs the entire season.

This would lead to her winning the Most Valuable Player (MVP) award. All of her hard work would finally pay off when the Storm went to the number one seed in the league, earning a double-bye in the semifinals.

The Storm finally won a series, moving to the Finals for the first time in eight years. The storm would beat the Washington Mystics and win their first championship with Breanna Stewart. She was overjoyed, especially after not being able to play in the championships in the last two years.

During the tournament, Stewart would average 25.7 points, 6 rebounds, 1.7 steals, and 3.7 assists. These numbers would help earn her the Finals MVP, making her the sixth player in the WNBA to win the Finals MVP and the league MVP in the same year. 2018 proved to be a very productive year for Breanna Stewart.

However, her promising WNBA career was about to come to a screeching halt in 2019.

Dealing With Adversity

Sadly, Stewart missed the entire 2019 season in the WNBA. She suffered an injury while playing in the 2019 EuroLeague Women's final on April 14th. On that same day, after a trip to the hospital, it was confirmed that she had torn her Achilles tendon.

She was flown home to the States the day after her injury. Stewart needed to go through surgery, which meant she would be suspended from the team. The WNBA had no inactive listing, so there was no way to keep her in that season and the Storm needed to have another player to fill her role. Stewart was frustrated and disappointed with how things were going.

While she was recovering, the WNBA made her a paid ambassador for the league. While she enjoyed representing the WNBA, Stewart realized that she was being paid more to be an ambassador than she was being paid to play the sport. The thought saddened her.

WNBA and Money

Breanna Stewart was making far less money than she deserved as a player considering her skill and background in the sport. It would not be until 2020 when the WNBA established the Collective Bargaining Agreement, allowing their players to make more money.

Women players were paid significantly less than their men counterparts in the NBA. Before the agreement was signed, most women rookie players made an average of $42,000 a year, while NBA players made about 13 times as much.

However, the new agreement would raise the average pay of women players to over $100,000. Still, it was nowhere near as much as the salary of NBA players.

Stewart was extremely disappointed that she was earning more money as an ambassador than as a professional basketball player—one who had participated in two All-Star games up to this point. Still, she loved the sport and was determined to continue playing.

BODY Issue
In 2018, Breanna Stewart was featured on the cover of a magazine. As she was being photographed for the magazine, she felt confident. She felt that she was reclaiming her body by posing for the photos.

She said that she spends a lot of time taking care of her body because she has always wanted to be in peak condition to play basketball. By taking care of herself, Stewart is able to perform at her best during games.

Additionally, having her pictures taken made her feel more confident. Stewart used to feel self-conscious about being taller than everyone else. However, the pictures allowed her to prove that she has finally embraced all of herself.

She truly understood her body and accepted herself. It was a moving moment for her and helped in further establishing her as a professional in the WNBA.

Returning to Basketball
Once Breana Stewart had recovered from the surgery on her Achilles, she was ready to return to the sport for the 2020 season.

It was July 2020 when she was allowed to make a return.

BOUNCING BACK

Stewart returned to the court; she had missed it. She would rejoin her teammates for training at the IMG Academy. Then she would earn another title with the Storm when she scored in another Finals MVP. She was also named the Sportsperson of the Year for her activism in her daily life.

Activism

Stewart showed her support to the Black Lives Matter movement after returning from her injury. She stood in front of the crowd and asked everyone to observe 26 seconds of silence for Breonna Taylor, the Black woman who was killed by the police in her apartment.

Stewart did so with the quiet confidence that she always seemed to display.

During this time, she would also use her platform in the WNBA to speak out against sexual abuse. Additionally, Stewart would begin to fight for gender pay equality. It seemed as though she had found her voice and was developing more confidence in herself.

As the WNBA's best player, she started realizing that she had the power to enforce good changes around her. Stewart would become dedicated to social justice during this time. She knew that it was important for her to point people toward the incredible stories of other women.

Stewart felt that women athletes deserve to have more fame. In her acceptance speech to the ESPYs, she stated that since everyone loves and supports the women in their lives, shouldn't everyone want to be a part of the change?

In 2018, she would team up with RAINN and was even named to the network's National Leadership Council. This gave her the opportunity to talk with other women about their experiences, giving her a platform to help survivors of abuse.

Continuing to Play Overseas
Breanna Stewart never wanted to take a break from basketball. In February of 2020, she signed up with the UMMC Ekaterinburg for their 2019 to 2020 Europe season. Then in November of 2020, she signed up with them again to continue playing the following year.

These experiences allowed her to meet new people and travel the world. Breanna Stewart took it as an opportunity to grow and learn more about the world around her. Plus, she was passionate about the sport and used her time across the seas to further improve her skills.

Another reason she decided to attend was the prospect of earning more income. Most WNBA players would play overseas when the U.S. completed its season; more time playing meant more money for the players, so the majority of them would participate.

For Breanna Stewart, she did not want to pass up these opportunities. It made financial sense to her, plus, she would get to test her skills further.

The EuroLeague is a very high, professional level in the world of basketball. Breanna Stewart saw it as an opportunity to earn more money but also as the perfect chance to test herself as a pro basketball player.

While overseas, Stewart had to push herself as hard as she could, despite the lingering effects of her injury. The Russian team consisted of at least six other All-Star WNBA players, meaning that she needed to work hard to keep up with everyone.

However, she felt her confidence returning during the experience. She was getting comfortable again on the court, right before the coronavirus pandemic put everything in the world of sports on hold.

Effects of the Pandemic
While the NBA had to shut down due to the pandemic, the WNBA only had to delay the start of their season. It started in July and all the fans were prevented from coming to the games. It was a weird feeling, but it needed to be done to protect people from getting sick.

The WNBA required that players go through a quarantine period before they can play. There were zero positive tests among the 139 women players, allowing them to play as long as they stayed isolated for the rest of the season.

However, Breanna Stewart would need to postpone her return to the WNBA. She stayed with her loving mother in their apartment during the highest points of the pandemic. To stay in shape, she lifted weights at home and rode an indoor bike every day.

Despite her life completely changing, she was happy to spend time at home with her mother. The two would relax and watch ESPN rewinds together. However, Stewart was itching to return to playing her favorite sport.

Sportsperson of the Year

Due to her activism and amazing performance before her injury, Breanna Stewart was chosen to be the Sportsperson of the Year. She had blossomed into a true professional and was receiving the recognition and awards she deserved for her efforts.

As a white player in a league dominated by mostly black players, she determined she was going to be an ally. Not many other players have taken the stances Stewart has or are as open and willing to be a part of activism like she is.

Stewart would go on to say that women players need to spend a lot of time convincing people that they are the best at their sport. And on top of that, people should watch them play. She took many different activism stances during this year, leading to her capturing the attention of Sports Illustrated, which knew she would need to be their Sportsperson for 2020.

The Future for Breanna Stewart

What will the next seasons bring for Breanna Stewart? She has grown so much since she was called "Bean" back in high school. Her parents are deeply proud of her and what she has accomplished.

For now, she is going to continue playing with the Seattle Storm, as well as traveling overseas during the States' off-seasons to continue playing basketball. The team has greatly benefited from having her on their side. Plus, all of her teammates love her and the silent confidence that she exudes.

Breanna Stewart's future looks brighter than ever right now. If you want to find out what she is planning to do next, it would be well worth your time to watch her! She will continue challenging herself and growing in her professional career.

Returning to Normal

After the pandemic halted her career, things are starting to return to normal for this All-Star. She will be returning soon and hasn't stopped playing like a true winner. Stewart felt that she had been away from the court for way too long.

Stewart felt that it was surreal to be back; she missed her teammates and the environment they created.

Changes in the League

A lot of changes have to be made in the league after the pandemic took place. Plus, the team was a lot different than what Stewart remembered. Some players had been moved to different teams and the Storm had plenty of rookies coming in.

Breanna Stewart was happy. The Storm was lucky to have plenty of healthy and fit players on their side. She felt that it was time again to shoot for another championship. Everyone was ready.

So, WHO IS BREANNA STEWART?

Breanna Stewart is a woman basketball player for the Seattle Storm. She has spent her entire life pushing herself to become stronger and accomplish many things in her basketball career. Plus, she has earned many titles and honors for herself through her hard work.

Stewart has always had a very supportive and loving family. It was their encouragement that helped her get to where she is. She realized that without their support she likely would not have made it so far in her professional basketball career.

Still, Stewart was a young girl who loved to play for fun back when she was young. That passion stayed with her through thick and thin, driving her to become the best player she could ever be. And while she is amazing now, she is still growing as long as she continues to push herself as hard as she can.

Stewart would go on to become an activist for many different causes in the WNBA; she joined the Black Lives Matter movement as well as feminist causes.

She believes that the wage gap between the WNBA and the NBA is ridiculous and continues to fight for equal pay. She has come a long way from the quiet, self-conscious girl who joined the league a few years ago.

Now, she is a strong and confident player, although her team feels that she is still quiet. Despite that, they now see how confident she is—there is a huge difference between Stewart now and the Stewart of a few years ago.

Overall, Stewart has achieved many of her goals and dreams. She had to work hard to get to where she is today, and she knows that she needs to continue working hard to meet all her new goals. No matter what she decides to do next, the WNBA and its fans will be keeping their eyes on her.

MORE FROM JACKSON CARTER BIOGRAPHIES

My goal is to spark the love of reading in young adults around the world. Too often children grow up thinking they hate reading because they are forced to read material they don't care about. To counter this we offer accessible, easy to read biographies about sportspeople that will give young adults the chance to fall in love with reading.

Go to the Website Below to Join Our Community

https://mailchi.mp/7cced1339ff6/jcbcommunity

Or Find Us on Facebook at

www.facebook.com/JacksonCarterBiographies

As a Member of Our Community You Will Receive:

First Notice of Newly Published Titles

Exclusive Discounts and Offers

Influence on the Next Book Topics

Don't miss out, join today and help spread the love of reading around the world!

Other Works By Jackson Carter Biographies

Made in the USA
Monee, IL
05 April 2025

15223071R00036